Sandhurst and Crowthorne

IN OLD PHOTOGRAPHS

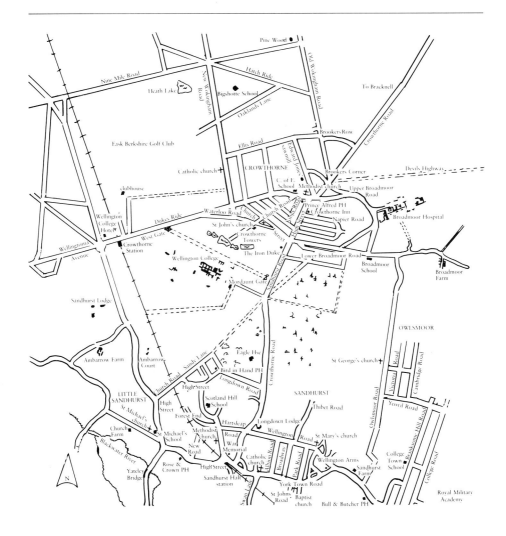

Sandhurst and Crowthorne

IN OLD PHOTOGRAPHS

Collected by KITTY DANCY
and ALLAN BROOKER

Alan Sutton Publishing Limited
Phoenix Mill · Far Thrupp
Stroud · Gloucestershire

BERKSHIRE BOOKS

First published 1992

Front cover picture: Lakes Stores, High Street, Crowthorne in the 1920s. Those of you who remember the shop will recall the aroma of dried apricots and roasting coffee. Left to right: Mr Keep, Mr Hampton, Mr Harris, Les Condick.

British Library Cataloguing in Publication Data

Dancy, Kitty
 Sandhurst and Crowthorne in Old Photographs
 I. Title II. Brooker, Allan
 942.29

ISBN 0-7509-0288-4

Typeset in 9/10 Sabon.
Typesetting and origination by
Alan Sutton Publishing Limited.
Printed in Great Britain by
WBC Print Ltd, Bridgend.

Contents

Introduction

Sandhurst

Sandhurst, derived from 'Sand', being the type of soil, and 'hurst', meaning wood, is situated in Berkshire, where the county meets the borders of Hampshire and Surrey, and was originally within the confines of Windsor Forest. Sandhurst is not mentioned in the Domesday Book but there is a written record in the exchequer rolls of Henry II (1175) when, for the 'Villata de Sandhurst', a receipt for the payment of one mark is recorded.

Just north of the built-up area of Sandhurst is the Devil's Highway, the Roman military road linking Londinium (London) with Calleva Atrebatum (Silchester). Nearby is a high point known as Caesar's Camp, which could have been a staging post for the Roman Legions; Roman pottery, tiles and coins have been found nearby. When the Romans departed the road was abandoned.

When William the Norman built Windsor Castle, the area became part of Royal Windsor Forest and everyone living within the confines was subject to the strict forest laws. There were special Forest Courts, the Swainmote was held three or four times a year, and severe sentences for poaching were passed. In 1723 the 'so called' Black Act became law. This punished local gangs of ruffians who had started out as poachers and become known as 'Wokingham Blacks' and who were terrorizing the district; the ring leaders were captured and convicted and hanged on four gibbets within the forest.

A survey carried out in the reign of King James I showed twenty-three houses in the area. Windsor Forest was divided into three Bailey Wicks and sixteen walks – Sandhurst Walk roughly corresponded to the pre-1894 Sandhurst; the last keeper of Sandhurst and Bigshotte Walks was Major General Cox who died in 1788 and is buried in Sandhurst churchyard.

William de Wanda, Dean of Sarum, visited Sandhurst in 1220 and saw the chapel of stone: 'Beautiful but not yet dedicated, a Font, but no burial ground, it belongs to the Chapel of Wokingham, John the Chaplain collects the tithes through Master Hannon, one mark and two pounds of wax, who sublet to John of Sherbourne for two marks'; John of Sherbourne is registered as the first incumbent of St Michael's church in 1222. The present church was built in 1853 under the direction of Mr G.E. Street and with generous financial support from

John Walters, the owner of the *The Times* newspaper, he also helped to fund the building of St Michael's School which is adjacent to the church.

The present Methodist church was opened on 2 May 1906 but there had been a Wesleyan chapel further up Scotland Hill and a Methodist school was opened in 1871 to accommodate 140 pupils (mixed) right on top of the hill. The Baptist chapel was erected in 1884 and is still situated on the corner of St John's Road but no longer referred to as Pigg's Cathedral (in acknowledgement of William Beechey Pigg, nick-named 'whopping big pigg' by local children, who had sold the site for the building of the chapel for £50). The Roman Catholic church was built in 1959 and the first service held on Christmas Eve 1959. The facilities, nowadays, are used for concerts and exhibitions by local organizations.

The Royal Military College was moved from Marlow to Sandhurst in 1812 and the College was opened that same year for the training of cadets to become officers in the British Army. Over the years the sports and social life of the RMC played a big part in the activities of the village and a walk through the lovely grounds and round the lake was taken for granted until 1974 when, for security reasons, the gates were closed. Special passes are now needed to enter the grounds. In 1912 the New College was opened, then the Staff College for the training of senior officers, and, more recently, the Victory College. The name Sandhurst became known world-wide. This brought an influx of people into the area, firstly to help with construction and, secondly, to work and give service to the new establishment. Farms, large country houses and estates developed, as well as shops and houses for the work force. The railway was constructed – the South Eastern and Chatham line came through in 1848 – but Sandhurst didn't have a local station until 1909 when Sandhurst Halt opened.

Wellington College was founded in 1859 as a memorial to the Duke of Wellington, the victor of Waterloo, and to form a school for the orphans of army officers. Broadmoor Criminal Lunatic Asylum opened in 1863. More information about these two establishments is given in the Crowthorne section of the introduction as they were included in the geographical area of Crowthorne when it became a separate civil parish in 1894.

By 1903 Sandhurst had a population of 5,565. Listed in Norman's *Directory* were farmers, gardeners, carpenters, builders, blacksmiths, bootmakers, butchers, dairymen, printers and painters, nurserymen and laundries, livery stables, carriers' cab proprietors, tailors and grocers, as well as ten pubs, all managing to make a living locally.

Sandhurst's population has continued to grow, and with the use of the car people commute over greater distances. Many of the farms and the large country house gardens have become housing estates, and the few large houses that remain have been converted into flats or nursing homes. The grounds of Snaprails and Ambarrow Court have become parks and the memorial fields in the centre of Sandhurst provide a recreational area that stretches down to the Blackwater River and to the Wish Stream separating Sandhurst from Hampshire and Surrey respectively.

Instead of all the small local shops, we now have superstores, Safeways, Marks and Spencers and Tescos with parking for over 2,000 cars. Many local organizations are still well supported: the annual Donkey Derby and the

Carnival Week, the Sandhurst Silver Band, the Women's Institute, the Gardening Club, the Social Club, the football clubs and Scouts and Guides, plus the excellent Day Centre for the elderly.

In 1974 Sandhurst Parish Council changed to a Town Council; thus there is a mayor of Sandhurst and a population of about 20,000. However, the wards, College Town, Owlsmoor, Central Sandhurst and Little Sandhurst still follow the old pattern of the village.

Crowthorne

Situated in Berkshire between Sandhurst and Bracknell, Crowthorne became an ecclesiastical parish in 1874 and, following the Act of Parliament which established secular Parish Councils, became a separate parish on 30 September 1894; prior to this it had been included in the parish of Sandhurst. The name Crowthorne figures in the Norden map of 1607 as the junction of three walks in the Windsor Forest: Sandhurst Walk, Bigshotte Walk, and Easthampstead Walk.

The population of the area grew with the establishment of Wellington College and Broadmoor Lunatic Asylum. Wellington College was founded as a national memorial to the Duke of Wellington, who died on 14 September 1852. An appeal was launched to set up a charitable institution in the form of a school to educate the orphans of army officers. The response to the appeal was good. Contributions and promises were received from many sources and by August 1853 £100,000 had been subscribed. All officers and other ranks of the British Army were required to subscribe a day's pay. The Queen granted a Charter which defined the scope and nature of the endowment:

> The Corporation is established for the providing out of funds at their disposal a College for the education and bringing up, maintaining and clothing of the children of deceased officers who have borne commissions in our Royal Army or in the Army of the East India Company and none others – and that such children shall be eligible as candidates without regard for their religious persuasion or creed provided they shall have been born in legal wedlock and in the estimate of the Governors shall be in the circumstances of need and that not more than three children of the same officer shall be admitted as scholars at the same time.

The Sandhurst site was chosen for a number of reasons. In the first place there was an abundance of building materials in the locality – bricks, sand, gravel and grit – while a good natural water supply was to hand. The railway ran close by and the area was open and healthy. There is little doubt that what clinched the deal was the offer, by Mr Robert Gibson of Sandhurst Lodge, of the 12-acre site within a few miles of the Royal Military College free of charge, with the possibility of purchasing a further 130 acres for £10 an acre. The governors purchased 120 acres in addition to the 12 free acres. A suitable architect, Mr John Shaw, was found to prepare a plan which was approved in 1855.

Queen Victoria laid the foundation stone on 2 June 1856. The first seventy-six boys arrived on 20 January 1859. The first headmaster was Revd Edward White Benson. The grounds of the College were landscaped under the supervision of Mr Menzies, formerly deputy ranger of Windsor Park. Wellington College has always had strong links with the military and the figures suggest that 10,700 boys passed through the College between 1859 and 1948, and of those 1,300 were to die in the service of their country.

The local railway station was opened on 10 February 1860. As the College had paid £500 towards the cost it was named 'Wellington College for Crowthorne', and that was its official designation until 17 June 1928 when it was renamed 'Crowthorne'.

Broadmoor Hospital, or Broadmoor Criminal Lunatic Asylum as it was originally called, was established following the Criminal Lunatic Act 1860. The first patients were received on 27 May 1863. The ground plan was based on two enclosures, 14 acres for men and 3½ for women, with the medical superintendent's house in between. In 1864 the possible causes of insanity were listed as: anxiety, epilepsy, intemperance, vice, poverty, religious excitement, fright, and exposure to hot climates. The Annual Report of 1877 gave a classifying list of crimes and sentences of those patients in the asylum totalling 481. Of these, 338 were detained for murder, attempted murder or manslaughter, 34 for arson, 21 for larceny, 19 for burglary and house-breaking, and a further 19 for insubordination – these were all soldiers. Following the escape of a patient named Straffen in 1951, a system of alarms has been installed in the area around the hospital; the siren sounds each Monday morning at 10 a.m.

Many local families have been connected through their work with Broadmoor or Wellington College for three or four generations. For, with the building of Wellington College and Broadmoor, many people were attracted to the area, both during the building and later, as staff or as shopkeepers catering for local needs. Spiritual needs were at first met by services held in people's homes but the building of churches soon became necessary. The parish church of St John the Baptist was consecrated on 5 May 1873. The building cost about £2,300, much of it raised by contributions and special gifts. Mr Lenny, who had been curate at Sandhurst, became the first vicar in 1874. The 'Iron Mission Room' at Owlsmoor went into use as a church and a school in 1880. The Methodist chapel was opened on Good Friday 1870. The land was given by Mr John Walter MP, the local benefactor, and the building cost £173 11s 2d. The existing Methodist church was built in 1898.

The Roman Catholic church was erected in 1909, a corrugated iron church built as a Chapel of Ease in New Wokingham Road. Father Daniel Boyle arrived in 1948 and was the inspiration for amassing huge sums of money for building and equipping the Catholic churches in Crowthorne and Sandhurst and the Catholic school.

A Baptist chapel was moved from Calcot and re-erected on a site in Crowthorne High Street and dedicated on 20 November 1918. It was decided to construct a permanent brick building in 1950 and, with financial aid from Miss Amy Hill, the building was ready for opening on 22 May 1954. It had been hoped Miss Hill would 'open the door' but she was too ill and died on 4 July that same year; she left a considerable sum of money to the church.

Broadmoor School in Crowthorne is as old as the hospital. In 1863 a note states eighteen children were of an age to attend school and that parents would be willing to pay according to their means. In 1904 Broadmoor School became a Berkshire County Council school and numbers have risen to over 170 pupils.

The Church of England School dates from 1875 and preserved aided status until 8 April 1958 when it became a County Council controlled school.

Edgbarrow Secondary Modern School opened in 1959 with 280 boys and girls in the first intake. They came from Sandhurst and Crowthorne and were children aged 11 years who had not been selected for grammar schools. As the population grew it was decided to build a second school in Sandhurst and this opened in 1969; eventually both schools became comprehensives. Part of Edgbarrow School has for many years been used as a community centre.

Many names from days gone by are still remembered locally: The Walter Recreation Ground, The Morgan Centre, Thomas Hunt, Bookseller, Printer and Bookbinder. The Crowthorne Picture House (H.G. Rainbow, manager) has long since gone. There is still The Iron Duke, the Prince Alfred, the Crowthorne Inn, and the Waterloo Hotel, but the site of the Wellington Hotel is replaced by houses. The East Berkshire Golf Club is still there as well as the old traders: Newmans for shoes, Watts for furnishing and Pearmain's Garage.

The population of the parish of Crowthorne in 1992 is about six thousand, with an overflow into Wokingham Without of another six thousand.

SECTION ONE

Royal Military Academy Sandhurst

Entrance to the Royal Military College Sandhurst from London Road.

The Terrace, Royal Military College, known locally as 'Tea Caddy Row'. It was used as family residences for senior staff at the College.

A view across the lake, Royal Military College, in 1915, showing the boat-house in the distance.

The Royal Military College, 1925, showing the parade ground and main entrance.

This picture, postmarked 20 July 1948, shows the tradition of the mounted horse being ridden up the steps to the Old College building at the end of the Passing-Out Parade which has been maintained for many years.

The New College Officers Mess, 10 May 1913, showing King George V, Queen Mary and Princess Victoria with senior officers and staff of the Royal Military College, now RMA Sandhurst. To the right of the King and Queen are Princess Mary, Mrs L.A.M. Stofford, Lady Bertha Dawkins, the Hon. Lady Haig; to the left of Princess Victoria are Earl Roberts, General Sir J.D.P. French, General Sir Douglas Haig.

This picture was taken before 1914 and shows the New College which was opened in 1912 with ground staff pulling the roller. Left to right: -?-, -?-, Harry Warner, Jim Foy, Jack Foy.

Pupils of the school for children of staff of RMC Sandhurst in 1897. For a number of years around this time there was a school for children between 3 and 7 years old, held in what is now the Museum of the Royal Military Academy.

Cricket ground, pavilion and gymnasium at the Royal Military College as they were in the 1920s.

Sports day at the RMC Sandhurst, 1923. Families gathered outside the cricket pavilion to watch and perhaps join in the day's events.

British Legion members in their thousands, each of the branches displaying their standards, on parade as they approach the Royal Military Academy (renamed after the Second World War), September 1956.

In September 1956 four hundred blue and yellow standards of the British Legion assembled in front of the RMA and dipped their standards as the bearer of the area standard, Mr G.E. Clarke, passes in front of them.

The drive, Royal Military College, remembered with pleasure by local people who used to have free access to the College grounds which are now closed for security reasons.

The altar of the Catholic chapel of Christ the King which was opened at the RMA Sandhurst in December 1948 by the Cardinal Archbishop of Westminster, Cardinal Griffin DD. The temple-like canopy over the altar was adapted from the grand entrance to the Old College building. Money was provided by corps and regiments of the British Army, Catholic schools and by the United Services Catholic Association.

SECTION TWO

College Town

Seeby & Son. For many years the Seeby family farmed the fields in College Town that lead down to the Blackwater River. The picture shows Mr Seeby in the door of his shop in the 1930s. The shop always had an array of flowers, fruit and vegetables, many grown by this local family who served Sandhurst so well down the years and to whom we owe the recently built Pastoral Centre near St Michael's church.

Pitchell's Stables, Yorktown Road, Sandhurst in the 1930s.

Oakfield Laundry, Branksome Hill Road, 1912, showing the staff, the laundry baskets and the transport vehicle, the side of which states that the laundry was awarded medals and diplomas at London and Liverpool exhibitions.

OAKFIELD LAUNDRY,

BRANKSOME HILL ROAD,

SANDHURST

for High Class and Economic

LAUNDRY SERVICE.

—————

'PHONE US !!

A collection of Cumnors. Back row, left to right: George, Charlie, Arthur. Middle row: Thomas, Sidney and Miriam (parents), Christopher. Front row: Harry, Edward, Richard. About 1902 this picture was sent to the royal family at Buckingham Palace, the response was the gift of £1 to each of the sons.

College Town Lads Club outside the Old Mission room, Branksome Hill Road, 1922–3. Back row, left to right: H. Leggett, B. Fowler, F. Knight, E. French, R. Cousins. Middle row: C. Boyd, P. Williams, Sid Hawkins, H. Pearce, A.J. Pearce, H. French, T. Hawkins, J. Carter.

Home Guard, College Town in the Second World War.

S.A. Stoner's shop, 1965. Situated in Yorktown Road, Stoner's was a newsagents and sweet shop, well used by local children on their way to school.

Sandhurst Carnival procession passing by The Nook and Pitman's newsagents, Yorktown Road, in 1934.

Silver Grill and College Town Stores, 1965.

Children on their way home from school rode happily through the floods of October 1956. Others were met by their parents and had to be carried home.

The Old Bull and Butcher public house, situated opposite the junction of the Owlsmoor Road, long since demolished and replaced by the present Bull and Butcher pub.

This picture of the Owlsmoor Road in 1939 shows it as a rural run that led to the gypsy encampment for which Owlsmoor was renowned. It has since been replaced by vast new housing estates, the Sandhurst Comprehensive School with nearly a thousand pupils, and Owlsmoor Primary School with over five hundred pupils.

Owlsmoor Stores, opened by Mr Brant of Owlsmoor in 1928.

Spooners Stream, Owlsmoor in 1938.

St George's church, Owlsmoor. 'The Iron Church' was built in 1880 and by 1885 there were about 190 souls in Owlsmoor, which later became part of Crowthorne parish. In 1973 the church was transferred back to the parish of Sandhurst. Owlsmoor now has its own vicar.

SECTION THREE
Central Sandhurst

Sandhurst Farm when it was owned by Mr and Mrs Wakefield, 1950–2. The farmhouse was standing in 1750 and may well be about fifty years older than that.

The Wellington Arms pub at the junction of Yorktown Road and Wellington Road, known for years as 'The Slip Inn' (you could slip in the door on one side and slip out the other on your way to and from work). William Purvey became landlord in 1891 and it stayed in the family for many years. They were proprietors, hiring out horse-drawn brakes and, later, the first local motorized taxi – a De Dion Bouton.

Yorktown Road in 1922, showing the shop that in 1992 is the Glass Centre. The houses are still there.

Sandhurst Football Team in the late 1940s. Back row, left to right: Alan Hannington, Ted Hutchings (secretary), Arthur Smith (trainer), Fred Turny, Dave Haxell, Jim Witman, Ken Razell, Sam Hutchings, Reg Dunn, Jimmy Nichol, Ron Clarke, Bobbie Mears, Malcolm Greenfield, Ernest Harrison. Front row: Bert Moore, ? Lewington, Paul Rideout, Tony Lee, Colonel Hardcastle (president), Sergeant Axford (chairman), George Billson, Jack Parker, Bill Greenfield (treasurer), Frank Roberts.

Sandhurst Fizzers Football Team in the early 1920s. Back row, left to right: Dick Hodge, George Wiseman, Bert James, Sid James, Eddie Watts, George Goddard, Bill Repton Baker, Jack Rush, Sam Benham. Front row: Bill Osbaldston (secretary), Jack Turner, Albie Final, Bill Ogbourne (in civvies), Bill Smith, Sid Rance, Fred Morgan, Jimmy David, Bill Final. Seated: Dibby Dayborn, -?-.

Donkey Derbys have been organized by the Sandhurst Roman Catholic church since 1966 to raise money for charities and the RC Parish Centre. Thousands come to watch and children compete to ride the winner in the Sandhurst Donkey Derby.

The Baptist church in 1979 at the junction of Yorktown Road and St John's Road. The chapel was erected in 1884 on a plot of land purchased for £50 from William Beechey Pigg, a local business man.

In 1956, when Allsworths Stores, then Does Stores, was completely surrounded by water, a platform of planks and crates was put down for customers to cross from the pavement to the entrance. The shop is now a garden centre.

Park Road, just a track across the field with The Homestead and a few other houses, looking towards Wellington Road. The road was not tarmacadamed until after the Second World War and the frontage owners had to pay so much a foot to cover the cost.

Interior of the old St Mary's church photographed in 1940 by Mr Fred Robinson who lived at Snaprails and had a very well-known photographic business in the High Street, Camberley.

The demolition of St Mary's church, 1962; a hall and small chapel have been built to replace the church.

View from the bedroom window of No. 15 Wellington Road, 1947, showing the harvest being gathered in. The field was part of Sandhurst Farm and next to Snaprails Estate. A few years later the houses of Wellington Close covered the field.

St Mary's church, Wellington Road, 1940. Notice the monkey puzzle tree which flourished there for many years.

Fancy dress party at Wellington Close, 2 June 1953, to celebrate the coronation of Queen Elizabeth II. Back row: on the stretcher, Alan Pinner; left to right: Wally Groves, Trisha Haines, Jilly Collins, Ann Newbold, Richard Hattam, Mary Roberts, Celia Cook, Micheline Hattam with Cliff Jones on lap, Pat Pinner, Wendy Hicks, Martin Hicks, Robbie Pinner, Kathleen Richardson, Jenny Walker, Marjorie Howard. Middle row: Christopher Robinson. Front row: Angela Groves, Cynthia Gillet, Carol Dillon, Rosemary Collins, Jackie Smith, Terry Dillon, Stuart Smith, Marie Townsend, Butch Newbold, Peter Hicks, Martin Hicks, -?-, Willie Townsend.

Victory party following the end of the war in May 1945. Children from Yorktown Road and Albion Road are gathered together by St Mary's church.

Snaprails Farm as it was about 1928. The old house is still there, surrounded by modern houses. The nearby grounds of Snaprails House are now a pleasant public park.

The Working Men's Club and hall was built in Wellington Road in the 1920s. Alterations have taken place over the years and it has now been renamed the Social Club.

Sandhurst Lawn Tennis Club, Wellington Road, 1930. Anyone for tennis? Certainly Edith Young and Bert Steward are doing their best on the doubles court. I wonder who was on the other side of the net?

Sandhurst Silver Band, 1920–1. Back row, left to right: Sid Evans, Horace Skillings, Fred Smith, Ernest Piper, Jess Roach, Ted Timms. Middle row: Harry Gore, Jack Daley, -?-, Taffy Williams, Fred Morgan, -?-, Mr Jeffreys, Will Jeffreys, Joe Final, Mr Skillings. Front row: Cliff Clarke, Bill Austin, Mr Johnson, Mr Bennellick, Mr Church, Mr F. Bennellick, Joe Evans, Mr Taylor. Seated: Dick Bird, Jack Bird.

Sandhurst Silver Band and supporters with the Rt. Hon. Randal Parsons, rector of
Sandhurst 1880–1921. Back row, left to right: Joe Foster, -?-, Arthur Payne, -?-, Mr Kent
(baker), Teddy James (newsagent), Mr Dullingham, Bill Austin, Herbert Watts (Registrar
of Births and Deaths), R. Cooper (coal merchant), -?-, Mr Arthur Harper (cycle shop).
Seated: Mr Shaw (head groundsman, RMC), -?-, the Rt. Hon. Randal Parsons, Mr
Bennellick (bandmaster), Joe Evans (head gardener, Snaprails). Front: Mr Johnson, Mr
Coombes.

Revd Mr Clayton, the curate in Sandhurst for many years, lived in Thibet Road and supported the local Scouts and the Bowling Club. The field opposite his house was used for Scout fêtes and local camps.

The view from Stapleton Villa, Wellington Road, showing the Silver Jubilee Carnival procession in 1935 with the local Scouts holding their banners high.

The Corner Stores, situated on the corner of Wellington Road and Albion Road. In the doorway waiting to welcome customers is Mr Greenfield. The shop is now closed.

Mr and Mrs Greenfield standing outside the Corner Stores which they ran for thirty-one years. The view shows Wellington Road tree lined, and the errand boy's bike leaning against the wall.

St Helen's House, situated on the left of the walls at the top of Wellington Road, has since been demolished.

The last days of St Helen's House, showing the demolition of the area before the building of St Helen's Crescent which replaced the house and garden in the 1960s.

Horse and cart driving up between the walls at the top of Wellington Road. There is now a one-way traffic flow system in this area.

Mrs Mills, whose husband made his fortune in the Australian gold-fields, enjoys the view at the back of Longdown Lodge. The garden of the estate is now covered with houses and the large house has been converted into flats.

SANDHURST
Grand National Steeple-Chase,
To be held DECEMBER 17th, 1894.

| First Race. | District Councils. | Gold Cup. |

PROBABLE STARTERS.	JOCKEYS.	BETTING.
Robert the Devil	R. Bunce	10 to 1 on
Collection Box	G. James	10 to 1 on
Granter	W. P. Pigg	5 to 1 on
Two Sticks	W. Farrer	10 to 1 against
The Duchess	Mrs. Orsborn.	50 to 1 against
Blue Funk	G. S. Harvey	100 to 1 against

| Second Race. | Sandhurst Parish Councils. | Hunt Cup. |

PROBABLE STARTERS.	JOCKEYS.	BETTING.
The Trooper	W. Bashford	20 to 1 against
Bones	A. Bown	10 to 1 on
Lather Brush	R. Bunce	10 to 1 on
Truth	T. Burrett	100 to 1 against
Black Diamond	R. Cooper	50 to 1 against
Sky Blue	Jesse Cox	20 to 1 against
Fir Apple	Josiah Cox	20 to 1 against
British Chop Stick	G. Cox	20 to 1 against
Brown Bow-Wow	N. Elphick	50 to 1 against
Tomato	H. Eyre	2 to 1 on
Knight	W. Farrer	25 to 1 against
Blind Man	W. Freuantle	5 to 1 on
Dough Puncher	A. Goddard	5 to 1 on
Stink Trap	J. Harrison	50 to 1 against
Cod Fish	S. Hawkins	2 to 1 against
Little Wonder	G. James	15 to 1 on
Account Book	J. Ledger	1000 to 30 against
Cucumber	G. Maddison	100 to 1 against
The Eagle	A. N. Malan	2 to 1 against
Hop Bitters	G. Melsome	25 to 1 against
Lady Godiva	Mrs. Orsborn	50 to 1 against
Silver King	W. B. Pigg	5 to 1 on
Lantern	J. Pitts	At no price
Straightforward	J. Rose	4 to 1 on
Physic	J. Russell	20 to 1 on
Whistle Pipe	T. Sheppard	1000 to 20 against
Wax	W. Taylor	scratched

Vote for the "Odds On" Candidates.

Sandhurst Grand National Steeple Chase to be held on 17 December 1894. These were the 'Runners' for the first election for councillors on the District and Parish Councils. It is interesting to note that a lady, Mrs Orsborn, was standing for election long before women in England had a vote.

The original members of Sandhurst Women's Institute. Supporters and performers of *Macbeth*, 11 May 1927. Back row, left to right: Mrs Monk Smith, Mrs Desborough, Mrs Wombwell, Miss M. Payne, Mrs Hayward, Mrs Young, Miss Jessie Evans, Miss E. Jeffreys, Mrs Stembridge. Middle row: Mrs Weston, Mrs Goswell, Mrs Filbie, Mrs Spratley, Miss Cove, Mrs Evans, Mrs Jeffreys, Mrs Blore, Mrs Alfred Payne. Front row: Miss Bandel, Miss Kerr, Mrs Johnson, Miss Marjorie Pearce, Miss Hazel Haywood, Miss Kerr, Miss Phyllis Johnson, Mrs Carter, Miss Ella Jeffrey, Miss Florence Young.

Sandhurst Women's Institute in fancy dress in 1928, complete with the Sandhurst WI banner. Back row, left to right: Mrs Spratley, Mrs Bigwood, Miss Betha Stembridge, Miss Marjorie Pierce, Miss Hayward. Middle row: Mrs Monksmith, Miss Kathleen Kelly, Mrs Hayward, Mrs Wombwell, Mrs Johnson, Mrs Evans, Mrs Bennett. Front row: Mrs Collins, Miss Florence Bigwood, Mrs Ackrill, Mrs Willis, Miss Florence Young, Mrs Steward, Mrs Blore, Mrs H. Steward, Mrs May, Mrs Carter.

Mrs Jeffreys with the Sandhurst Women's Institute birthday cake which she had made and decorated with the red and green colours of the National Women's Institute 1916–37.

The Sandhurst Women's Institute was founded in 1919. This picture shows the netball team in April 1934. Left to right: Miss E. Johnson, Miss Betty Batts, Mrs Trench, Miss P. Johnson, Miss Blore, Miss E. Jeffreys, Miss C. France.

Albion Road in 1911 looking towards Wellington Road; the houses on the left are still there in 1992. Behind the trees on the right was Gothic Cottage, now replaced by flats.

Yorktown Road from the junction with Albion Road, looking towards the junction with Swan Lane and on to Sandhurst Halt railway station.

The ford in the Blackwater River, looking towards Sandhurst, 27 November 1911. Wisemans Farm can be seen in the distance.

A view of the footbridge across the Blackwater River that leads from Sandhurst to Darby Green, 20 September 1960.

Lakes Stores, provisions merchants and family grocers, 1930s, situated in Yorktown Road, to the right of where Barclays Banks is now. Bert Keep is standing in the doorway.

Roman Catholic church of the Immaculate Conception in the centre of Sandhurst and used for the first time on Christmas Eve, 1959. With the aid of local fund raising many additions have been completed, including a community hall and the belfry and clock that can be seen in the picture.

A view of Yorktown Road on 9 July 1916, showing Teddy James' shop, later Strattons, and looking towards the New Inn with the railway line on the left. The card is marked 'Newtown Sandhurst', but Newtown Road is to the right just before the view starts. The first shop on the right has a sign that says 'C. Harper'. It was originally a cycle shop where you could have your cycle repaired for ninepence.

Crowthorne Road, Sandhurst. How long ago would it have been that a mother could push a baby in a pram up the centre of Crowthorne Road? Those were the days of the rural parish of Sandhurst.

A view from Sandhurst Halt railway station of the unveiling of the Sandhurst War Memorial in honour of the men who fought in the First World War. The site had been donated by the Majendie family who lived on the Warren Estate; the house has since been demolished and the estate covered with houses. The War Memorial was moved to a site near the Community Centre in 1983 to avoid traffic congestion when the Memorial Service was held.

Scotland Hill, Sandhurst, viewed from the bend under the railway arch. The card is post-marked 24 September 1917.

The Wesleyan chapel, Scotland Hill, Sandhurst, was opened 2 May 1906, following a gift of land by Dr J. Russell, a valued friend of the Methodists in the early days of the century.

St Michael's Club, Sandhurst, 9 January 1920. The club was built in the 1880s with the support of wealthy people in the village to encourage social activities for the folk who lived and worked locally. It was well used until the new Working Men's Club was built in Wellington Road in the 1920s.

The well in Scotland Hill, erected by Mrs Blakeley of Forest End as a memorial to Harriet Walker Vyvan Connell, also of Forest End, who died August 1874. The picture is dated 5 July 1921.

An elderly couple in the doorway of Dawn Cottage, Scotland Hill, Sandhurst.

The crossroads by Fourways, Sandhurst, 1908. Down the road are two ladies standing by the well and near the hedge are Mr and Mrs Anderson with their daughter, Annie.

Steam train (the 'Continental') in Sandhurst Halt, passing through Sandhurst at 1.34 (2 minutes late) on Friday 8 April 1948 at a speed of 65 m.p.h. The train of GWR coaches is pulled by 2–6–0, No. 31804. Standing on the platform is Bill Maycock, the well-remembered stationmaster of days gone by.

Sandhurst Halt opened in 1909. The people on the platform are waiting for one of the first trains to call there.

Staff at Sandhurst Halt railway station in 1912.

The wooden bridge across the railway line, linking the footpath from Fourways to Ackrills Corner. Postmarked 12 August 1924.

Sandhurst Women's Institute float, Sandhurst Carnival, 1951. Left to right: Ciss Cousins, Ruth Paice, Mrs Harvey, Barbara Jones, Mrs Kirkham, Betha Green, Kitty Dancy.

SECTION FOUR
Little Sandhurst

A view of the High Street looking towards the railway arch, 5 August 1919. The Home and Colonial butchers shop with the errand boy's bike outside is today 'Exclusive Fireplaces'.

Sandhurst Mills, 1920, situated opposite Caves Farm, High Street, Sandhurst. Mr English and Mr Joe Cox are ready for work.

T. T. ENGLISH,

Sandhurst Mills,

SANDHURST———BERKS.

Contractors to H.M. Government.

Millers & Corn Merchants, Poultry & Cattle Food Specialists.

Tel. Yateley $\frac{218}{219}$ 2 lines.

Advertisement for Sandhurst Mills.

In the 1950s Lilyan's the hairdressers was situated next to the Dukes Head public house in what had in days gone by been a bakery but has now been demolished for a car park.

The Rose and Crown, Sandhurst's oldest public house, 30 September 1906. An alehouse licence was granted to Mrs Hannah Geale in 1742. The workmen are standing outside the forge owned by C. Giles. There was a forge next to the Rose and Crown for many years.

'The Handystore' in the High Street, Sandhurst, at the bottom of New Road, 12 June 1965.

A view of New Road, Sandhurst, 31 July 1906. Many families are coming out of their homes to be part of the picture. A family called Englefield lived in the house on the right.

Cornish's Shop, High Street, Sandhurst, showing Miss Dolly Cornish with little girl, Elsa, and a very clear advert for Liptons Tea.

View from The Cedars, the home of the Mason family, across Rectory Field towards St Michael's School. A snow scene in February 1937.

This snow scene on 25 April 1908 shows the bend in the road of High Street, Sandhurst, with The Cedars visible above the hedge on the right.

Rivermead House and stables just before it was demolished in 1986. It was situated near Yateley Lane and had been used as the Railway Tavern in the 1850s when the South Eastern and Chatham Railway was being constructed through Sandhurst.

Rectory Cottages, 1979. This very old building was converted from the Rectory Farm and is now surrounded by St Michael's housing estate. When the old barn was demolished a brick dated 1560 was found.

View of the Blackwater River from Yateley Bridge looking towards St Michael's church, Sandhurst.

The procession, led by Sandhurst Silver Band, marches past Rectory Cottages at the junction of Yateley Lane, 1909.

St Michael's School, Sandhurst, built in 1863. This picture shows the school and the head-teacher's house plus additional buildings erected at a later date. It is now used as a primary school.

Special Constables, Sandhurst Police, 1938. Back row: Bert Simpson, -?-, George Sherwood, Charlie Brant, Bert Provins, Bill Cornish. Middle row: Eddie Goddard, Bert Bandel, Harold Hedges, Tom Willis, Bill Greenfield, -?- , Bert Keep. Front row: -?-, Harry Rogers, Albert Johnson, -?-, -?-, Sgt. Axford, Mr Mossman, Sam Mason.

Even the fire brigade turned out when Sandhurst church held its Jubilee celebrations in 1905. Gentlemen donned their 'Sunday Best' and put carnations in their buttonholes, while the women, not to be outdone, put on their smartest hats.

St Michael's church, Sandhurst. The view across the churchyard to the south entrance. This church was built in 1853 under the direction of Mr G.E. Street.

Interior of St Michael's parish church, Sandhurst, looking towards the altar, 1910.

The lych-gate of St Michael's church. The rectory is on the opposite side of the main road.

The Old Rectory, Sandhurst, was built opposite the site of St Michael's parish church on the Sandhurst to Wokingham main road. It was demolished in 1956 and replaced with a modern, smaller rectory on the same site.

Ryefield House was the home of Mr Toye, a master at Wellington College. Mrs Toye was the first president of Sandhurst Women's Institute in 1919. The house and grounds are near St Michael's church.

The Sandhurst Women's Institute's 'Fashion down the Ages', 1951, on the steps of Ryefield, home of Lady Burdett. Back row: Jennifer Burdett, Miss Blakiston, Barbara Jones, Lady Burdett, Mrs Score. Fourth row: Mrs Kirkham, Mrs Cousins, Betty Reid, Mrs Jeffries, Mrs Busby, Alice Johnson. Third row: Ina Jones, Mrs Jones. Second row: Linda Jones, Mrs Harvey, -?-, Mrs Batts, -?-, Lorna Jones. Front row: Ruth Paice (seated), Virginia Mason, Kitty Dancy, Mrs Lockwood, Betha Green.

This is the notice of the sale of Ambarrow Court, Thursday 24 November 1932 at 3 p.m. precisely.

Ambarrow Court, 1887. This photograph belonged to Colonel Harvey. Colonel and Mrs Harvey lived at Ambarrow Court for many years and played a great part in the life of Sandhurst. The colonel was a local Justice of the Peace.

Ambarrow Lodge gate entrance, 1932. This led to Ambarrow Court. Both the lodge and the large house have been demolished but the grounds are well maintained as an open park and nature walk area in the care of the local council.

Apple Tree Cottages, 1932. These were linked to Ambarrow Court, the home of Colonel and Mrs Harvey, which was just down the road. When Mrs Harvey died in 1932, Mr Provins, the coachman, bought the two cottages at a public auction for £250; his daughter lived in one of the cottages until she died in 1985.

Ambarrow Farm Dairy. At one time ninety-six cows were being milked every day on this farm and milk-floats were delivering milk locally twice a day. There were no fridges so milk went sour quickly in warm weather.

Harvesting the field near the Blackwater River with Ambarrow Farm in the background, 1887. The branches on the backs of the horses served to ward off the flies. Gravel pits now cover this area.

Sir William Farrer, solicitor to Queen Victoria, who resided at Sandhurst Lodge from about 1880 until he died in 1911. A lovely garden was developed, which included a pond heated by a gas system from the house so that exotic water plants could be grown.

Aerial view of Sandhurst Lodge showing the house and grounds as it used to be. In recent years it has been converted into flats but the building and grounds are well cared for.

Coronation party at Forest End, Little Sandhurst, 2 June 1953.

A view of Sandy Lane, Little Sandhurst, in 1885. The thatched cottage owned by Wellington College has since been demolished.

A view of High Street, Little Sandhurst, in the early 1900s.

Five teachers from Scotland Hill School, 1938. Back row: Mr Ron Tovey, Mr Curtis. Front row: Miss Mayers, Miss Barrett, Miss Cone.

VE Day party in 1945 gathering in Little Sandhurst outside Napper's shop before going on to the Fox and Hounds to celebrate the end of the war in Europe.

A bonfire to celebrate the coronation in 1911, believed to be on the ground opposite Hancombe Road, Little Sandhurst. Dave Cripps is second from the left; Will Sharman is second from the right.

All dressed up for a children's party at Cock-a-Dobby about 1936. Bert Simpson is on the right with his medals up.

A view of High Street, Little Sandhurst, looking from Napper's stores towards Mount Pleasant with the Bird in Hand just over the hill.

'Longdown Meadow' was the title of this picture in the Kempthorne album in 1887. It is possible that the area later came to be used as Eagle House School playing fields.

Although entitled Eagle House, Crowthorne, the house is, in fact, situated in Sandhurst. It was at one time the home of Dr Russell but then became a preparatory school linked to Wellington College. This picture was taken about 1920.

SECTION FIVE
Crowthorne

Wellingtonia Avenue, 21 June 1932, planted in 1863 on instructions from John Walter III of Bearwood. A view from The Ridges looking towards Crowthorne.

The Crowthorne Girls Friendly Society, August 1934. They met once a week at Barracane, Wellington College and the fee was a penny a week. It was first run by Miss Cautley and later by Miss Booth.

Wellington College Hotel, situated near the railway station, now demolished and replaced by a housing estate.

The sign at the railway station says it all. The station was built to serve Wellington College in 1860 and there were originally eight members of staff. Today it is unmanned and called Crowthorne station.

Wellington College railway station with the South Eastern and Chatham Railway steam train, a class F1 A4–4–0 No. 1333. It was renamed Crowthorne station in 1928 but the sign remained until the beginning of the Second World War.

Aerial view of Crowthorne station and beyond in June 1936.

Shops near Wellington College station, 1885.

By 1908 the line of shops near Wellington College railway station had grown considerably.

East Berkshire Golf Club, Crowthorne, 1932. The club is situated at the end of Ravenswood Avenue.

Wicket Gate, Wellington College, 18 September 1912. The path led to the W.H. Smith shop and so became known as Smith's Path.

The West Gate entrance to Wellington College, 1929. A few years ago the elaborate wrought-iron section across the top of the gate was damaged by a lorry and had to be removed. The West Gate was named after the West family.

The front entrance to Wellington College in 1906.

WELLINGTON COLLEGE, SANDHURST.——Mr. John Shaw, Architect.

An engraving of Wellington College, Sandhurst, in 1856, before there was a named village of Crowthorne. It also gives the name of the architect as Mr John Shaw. There are no towers on the engraving but they are included in the ultimate design.

Speech Day, Wellington College, 1904. On the roof to the right of the clock tower a photographer is ready to record the events of the day when King Edward VII visited the college.

Wellington College front quadrangle in 1908.

The view of Wellington College south front in 1906.

Interior of a Wellington College boy's room. The partitions have now been removed to form an extended dormitory.

The Boys' Library, Wellington College, showing busts of various members of staff that have served the college through the years, together with royal founders including Queen Victoria and Prince Albert.

The indoor swimming baths, Wellington College, 1890. These were destroyed in a fire in 1992.

The old gymnasium, Wellington College, 1885.

The chapel, Wellington College. Prince Albert laid the foundation stone in 1861 only months before his death from typhoid. It was consecrated by Bishop Wilberforce of Oxford in 1863. The additional aisle is named after the first master, Dr E.W. Benson.

The interior of Wellington College chapel in 1906. The organ case in the north aisle has been replaced by the Lutyens Memorial, dedicated to the fallen of the First World War.

The garden party at Saunders House, Wellington College, which was renamed Benson House in 1914.

The Pavilion, Wellington College, 1906. This is situated on the main cricket field known as the 'Turf'.

View across Swan Lake to Wellington College, 24 July 1908. This is the largest of three lakes.

Wellington College domestic and work staff football team (1925) most of whom lived in Little Sandhurst. Back row, left to right: Mr Bennett, Mr James, Mr Long, Mr Morgan, Mr Ellis, Mr Bennett. Front row: Mr Shepherd, Mr Edwards, Mr Smith, Mr Newall, Mr Shepherd, Mr Clarke, Mr Austin, Mr Rogers.

The White Bridge, Wellington College, 5 April 1909. The path winds towards the College from The Towers and Greystokes on the Waterloo Road.

G.A. Kempthorne, from the Kempthorne album in the Wellington College archives.

A view near Wellington College, 10 January 1907, showing a lady taking a rest after a walk through the woods.

The grounds of Wellington College in 1915, showing the boundary gate. The path led to the White Bridge.

Aerial view of Wellington College, Crowthorne.

Wellesley Villas, Crowthorne, 1887.

The Mordaunt Gate, Wellington College, 1929, given by Mr Eustace Mordaunt, an Old Wellingtonian and governor.

A view of the West Gate, Wellington College, angled to look up Dukes Ride as it was in 1929.

A view further along Dukes Ride where the road forks to Waterloo Road as it looked in 1915.

The Waterloo Hotel, showing the main entrance from Waterloo Road, was used by visitors to Wellington College and is still flourishing today.

Members of the Crowthorne Red Cross, 1917. The Crowthorne Red Cross was formed on 19 April 1911 by Miss L.E. Monck of Aldworth House, Crowthorne, who is sitting in the centre of the front row.

The Towers School, Wellington College, 1909. The school was established as a preparatory school in 1867 and built in Waterloo Road, Crowthorne. It was demolished in 1938.

The parish church Christmas party at Pinefields in Waterloo Road. The Revd Mr Nugee is standing in the centre with flags flying overhead.

St John's Club Christmas party, 1946, also held at Pinefields.

Crowthorne parish church, where Mrs Walter laid the cornerstone, 27 September 1872. The church was consecrated, with great ceremony, by the Bishop of Oxford on 7 May 1873.

A view of the interior of Crowthorne parish church in 1907. The original cost of building the church was £1,934 19s and the money was raised through public subscriptions.

IN MEMORY OF
THOSE WHO GAVE THEIR
LIVES IN THE WAR
1939-1945

JAMES R. CARTER
REGINALD E. COTTERELL
ROBERT C. FOREST
MYRTLE D. GOLDSWORTHY
née PARTRIDGE
WILLIAM A. HANDS
VICTOR J. HALE
ROBERT HOLDAWAY
ALBERT W. JUSTICE
ALAN W. KER
ARTHUR R. LEWINGTON
ROBERT P. LONGDEN
HERBERT W. NORTH
EDWARD W. NORTH
WALTER E. NUNN
JOHN F. PAPWORTH
ALFRED G. POLDEN
JAMES D. REASON
WILLIAM R. REASON
FREDERICK W. RICHARDS
ANTHONY G. RICKCORD
JOHN S. RICKCORD
LEWIS O. SCUFFLE
JOHN L. TYLEY
ARTHUR J. WATKINS

The memorial to those who gave their lives in the Second World War was erected in Crowthorne parish churchyard and dedicated on 30 May 1953.

Crowthorne parish church, 1907, viewed from Church Street with Waterloo Road to the left.

A view of the roads around the church in 1886 showing the development of shops in Church Street, Crowthorne.

Church Street, Crowthorne, showing people doing their shopping in 1906.

Church Street, Crowthorne, 1906, is similar to the previous card but taken from a different angle.

The Garth Hunt meeting at The Iron Duke, Crowthorne.

Crowthorne Brownies outside The Iron Duke in 1922. Brown Owl: Miss M. Simmonds. Others named in the picture are: Hazel Fullbrook, Ethel Nunn, Jean Phillips, Connie Talmage, Rene Hallett, Annie Beacham, Margery Duponde, Connie Lovick, Connie Brooker, Joyce Condick, Rene Parker, Ena Watkins.

Crowthorne Cubs, 1950. The adults are, left to right: Mrs Levere, Mr B. Clayton, Mr Alan Gostick. On his left is Scout Brian Hallett.

The corner of High Street and Church Street, Crowthorne, 1886.

A view of Crowthorne High Street in 1921 showing the old chemists shop on the right and the sign for The Iron Duke on the left.

A view of the bottom of the High Street looking towards the road that leads to Sandhurst, 30 June 1905.

Crowthorne children around the maypole on the Morgan recreation ground, celebrating the coronation of King George V in June 1911. Back row, left to right: Victor Woodison, Gladys Grig, Ronald Golden, Dorothy Blunden, Cyril Sworder. Front row: Phyllis Hatfield, Roy Lightfoot, Ivy Allum, Fred Smith, Francis Golding, Charlie Bell.

Members of the Crowthorne Wednesday Football Club, 1920–2.

Members of the Crowthorne Saturday Football Club, 1921–2.

Bell's shop, Crowthorne High Street, was at one time a temporary church situated on the other side of the road where the fire station is now.

Newman's shoe shop and saddlery in 1905, showing the cart which went round the local villages collecting shoes for repair. The shop was to the right of Barclays Bank in Crowthorne High Street but has now been demolished.

High Street, Crowthorne. On the left are the premises of Davis the watchmaker, and on the right, Swains the greengrocer and other shops on the road that goes to Sandhurst.

Crowthorne Women's Institute drama members dressed for a play that was produced at the British Legion Hall, Wellington Road, in 1955.

Members of Crowthorne Women's Institute, 1930, taking part in the play *The Milk Maids*. Back row, left to right: Margaret Ison, Joan Ison, Mrs Robins, Mrs Fullbrook, Phyllis Lemmy, Barbara Lemmy, Margaret Noakes. Front row: Mrs Yaxley, Mrs Condick, Gladys Rich, Miss Hull, Miss Davis, Mrs Watts.

High Street Junction, Cambridge Road, 14 May 1914. Lovicks Corner is on the left.

Come for a 'Charabanc' ride with Mr B. Lovick driving the Lovick's coach.

Mr H. Woods, the driver, is southbound. One of the stately 'Charabancs' leaving Crowthorne on a seaside outing in 1919 at 12 m.p.h. The occupants were seldom in danger of losing their hats at that speed.

Upper High Street, Crowthorne. The white building on the right is the Crowthorne Inn at the junction of Napier Road. The whole highway is verdant with trees of which there are none surviving today. Note the donkey and cart being led up the road – no traffic humps!

Motorized traffic beginning to flow in Crowthorne High Street. Exide batteries and Star cigarettes are advertised outside Lawrence's newsagents and a sign says 'You may telephone from here'.

Hatfield, cycle dealer of Crowthorne, displaying the bicycles in the 1951 carnival. Each one is ridden by a member of the Hatfield family.

A view from the roof of Hatfield's shop of the 1935 carnival procession proceeding down the High Street towards the Prince Alfred.

Motor engineer H.G. Davis. Notice the bicycle displayed on the roof with the sign saying 'Garage and Cars for Hire'.

This notice came up on the screen of the local cinema and says it all!

Hatfield Cycles, Fishing Tackle and Insurance and the Regular petrol pump. This shop was previously Davis Cycle Shop but when Miss Davis married Mr Hatfield the name of the shop changed.

Pearmain's Garage, *c.* 1923–5, with Frank and Ken Pearmain standing outside.

Pearmain's Garage, motor and cycle engineers, with their cars standing in the High Street. The cars were both Austin 20s; Mr Pearmain owned the front one and the other belonged to his son, Ken.

High Street, Crowthorne in 1903. Two of the children on the left of the picture are Ted Lloyd and his sister.

Mr Reg Vaughan, who built the iron railing for Talbot House, Wellington College, in 1935.

The junction of the High Street and Dukes Ride showing the Prince Alfred public house. After heavy rain ponds used to form on the open land in the foreground.

Dukes Ride, 1926, showing the Methodist church, Crowthorne, which opened in 1898.

A time capsule was discovered buried in the wall of the Methodist church when the builders were adding an extension to the church in July 1984. The capsule contained three newspapers of 1898, a magazine and two coins (one a silver threepenny piece and the other a penny piece).

Crowthorne Methodist Youth Club, 1958–9. Among them are, back row, left to right: Nigel Elston, John Spiller, Trevor Woodage, David Asselbrough, Kay Daniel, Colin Bennett, Valerie Griffiths, -?-, -?-, Sue Ernie, Sylvia Kingham, -?-. Middle row: Brian Cowley, Les Hurdle, Sylvia Bird, -?-, -?-, Colin Godwin. Front row: Mrs Asselbrough, Tommy Hayes, Mabel Jones, -?-, Doreen Tye, Pam Collins, Hillary Bell, Moira Griffiths, Mr Asselbrough, Fred Bird.

Dukes Ride, Crowthorne, 1926, showing the post office adjacent to the Methodist church.

Oddfellows Christmas party, 1954, held at the Methodist church hall.

Puck Dancers, run by Miss Miriam Napier-Jones, Bessie Robinson and Doreen Caine, in the Silver Jubilee Carnival procession in 1935. Miss Napier-Jones was a professional stage dancer who started lessons for the girls in the village once a week on Wednesday nights; they were awarded different coloured sashes in order of merit. A Christmas concert was held in the parish hall. The group was formed in the 1920s and ran until the start of the Second World War.

Puck Dancers, 1922. Back row, left to right: Connie Talmage, Ivy Levington, Kathleen Yaxley, May Watts, Doreen Caine, Bessie Robinson, Marjorie Robins, Enid Cottrel, Nora Collet, Queeny Cox, -?-, Evelyn Singer, Mara Levington, Joyce Condick. Middle row: Cis Yaxley, Mary Wilson, Muriel Watts, Evelyn Collet, Ivy Bacon, Lena Speed, Marjorie Condick, Flossie Nunn, Laura Bennellick, Madge Hurdle. Front row: ? Macniece, Ethel Nunn, Dora Payne, Rene Hallet, Ethel Taylor, Nancy Street, Maggie Howard, Ena Watkins, Crystal Howard, Pearl Vaughan.

Crowthorne Church of England schoolteachers, 1927–8. Back row, left to right: Miss Hannington, Miss Newman, Miss Burton, Mr Ossie Hughes, Miss Nunn, Miss Annetts, Mrs Lockhart. Front row: Miss Maud Green, Mr Goodband, Canon Coleridge, Miss Booth, Miss Goddard.

Class V, Church of England School, 1921–2. Top row, left to right: Arthur Lloyd, Cecil Jaycock, Max Dewey, Jack Brooker, John Welsh, Kenneth Over, Nelson Smith, George Donnelly, Jack White, ? Ives. Second row: Lillian Slarke, Cecil Dewpond, Peter Hallet, Tom Wheeler, Edward Brooker, -?-, Jack Lovick, Cecil Reason, Monty Packworth, Edith Mason, Laura Bennellick. Third row: Pearl Vaughan, Marjory Condick, Ann Beecham, Edna Hallet, Agnes Hannington, Ciss Yaxley, Evelyn Collet, Kathleen Penny. Fourth row: Stan North, Alfred Lewington, Charlie Howlet, George Gilbert, Harold Pearmain, Freddy Chapman, Roy Trendle. Fifth row: Vic Hurdle, Arthur Ives, Bob Ward, Cecil Hallet, Tom Ward, John Bryan, Willie Lloyd.

Bigshotte Rayles Preparatory School dates from 1895, and in 1973 Wellington College assumed responsibility for the school.

The Roman Catholic church, New Wokingham Road, Crowthorne, was erected in 1909 and replaced by a brick building in 1960.

Interior of the Roman Catholic church of the Holy Ghost in its early days.

Up the drive of Pinewood in 1910, showing the patients' accommodation, with windows open so that the Open Air Sanatorium had the full benefit of the pine-laden air.

The Lodge entrance gate, Pinewood in 1909. This was the London Open Air Sanatorium.

A group of people enjoying a fête at Pinewood in the 1920s.

Miss Reeves standing outside the shop which she started. It was situated on the corner of Hatch Ride and Old Wokingham Road.

The Pine Woods, Crowthorne, showing the road which in 1910 led through the woods to Bracknell. It still does today but now there is a large roundabout to negotiate at this point.

The road junction at the end of Crowthorne High Street, showing Upper Broadmoor Road and the road to Bracknell that nowadays goes past Lightfoot's Garage.

Edward Jones' timbermill in Pinewood Avenue in the 1920s.

The workforce of Edward Jones' timbermill in the 1920s. Left to right: W. Johnston, Edward Jones (the owner), Bert Dale, W. Seymore, Mr Percy, E. Fisher, F. Milam, T. Day, F. Watts, J. Corduroy, and the dog, Mick.

Edward Jones' timberyard in the 1920s. The church spire is visible above the trees as well as the back of Ives' shop which faced down the High Street.

Edward Jones' sawmills in the 1920s. The workmen are standing in front of the massive machinery which was the power source for the timberyard. Left to right: -?-, Ted Jones, Bert Dale, Ernie Fisher, Frank Milam, Tom Day, Jim Herridge.

Forest Road, Crowthorne, showing Mr J.F. Reely with his grandson in the pram. The Postmark is 1915 but, from family knowledge of the baby, the picture was taken in 1912.

Upper Broadmoor Road, Crowthorne led from the junction by the Prince Alfred pub, past the White City, which is where some of the Broadmoor staff lived, and on to Broadmoor Criminal Lunatic Asylum.

The road passing the staff terrace to the front entrance of Broadmoor Asylum, showing the trees that are no longer there.

The imposing entrance to the Broadmoor Criminal Lunatic Asylum, Crowthorne, which gave employment to many local people.

The female wing of Broadmoor was built on an enclosure of 3¹/₂ acres and the first super-intendent was Dr John Meyer (1863–70). His first patients were ninety-five women who arrived in May 1863.

Male quarters, Broadmoor, built on an enclosure of 14 acres. The labour force came mainly from prisoners at Parkhurst on the Isle of Wight. The first male patients came in 1864 from Fisherton House and Bethlem Hospital.

The staff of Broadmoor Hospital in 1929. We have named as many as the men as we could. Back row, left to right: Mr Tye, Mr F. Lewis, Mr R. Webber, Mr G. West, Mr Denton, -?-, Mr Mansbridge, Mr Carter, -?-, Mr Druce, Mr Paine, Mr Boreman, Mr Bennett, Mr Page. Second row: Mr G. Justice, -?-, Mr R. Iliffe, Mr M. Harrison, Mr W. Tyler, -?-, Mr W. Tott, Mr F. Smith, Mr Hawkins, Mr A. Locking, Mr W. Keen, Mr J. Dixon. Third row: Mr J. Frazer, Mr F. Bovington, Mr Druce, -?-, Mr Smith, Mr Newson, Mr G. Gee, Mr Bullock, Mr H. Hayward, Mr Wilkins, Mr C. Jacock, Mr Illingsworth, Mr Byrn, Mr Evans, Mr Hudson. Fourth row: Mr G. Gaiter, Mr Richards, Mr Waite, Mr Searle, Mr J. Godwin, - ?-, Mr Roy Street, -?-, Mr B. Bailey, Mr F. Telling, Mr Ingliss, -?-, Mr Parson, Mr H. Freeman, Mr Brant, Mr Bennett, Mr Clacy, Mr Smith, -?-, Mr J. Farr, Mr Illingsworth, Mr E. Boyers, -?-, -?-. Fifth row: Mr J. Johnson, Mr Pinecot, Mr Hurnal, Mr G. Owen, Mr Dovey, Mr Howard, Mr T. Clarke, Mr Woodman, Mr Headley Rich, Reverend Whiteley, Dr Hopwood, Dr Fullerton, Dr Knox, Mr Wigley, Mr Penson, Mr W. Owen, Mr Leadbetter, Mr Tapper, Mr Robertson, Mr W. Hull, Mr Dance, Mr Dance, Mr D. Evans. Sixth row: Mr C. Lamdon, Mr F. Scott, Mr W. Hale, Mr Beales, Mr L. Tanner, Mr T. Leckaby, Mr F.J. Bennellick, Mr Thrower, Mr Gordon, Mr A. Pearce, Mr F. Pearce, Mr J. Watts, Mr W. Smith, Mr A. Ingliss, Mr J. Gater, Mr Lawrence, Mr Gibbons, Mr West, Mr Scarnell.

A view from the south of Broadmoor Lunatic Asylum in the 1860s.

Broadmoor Asylum showing the security wall and some of the staff houses, most of which have now gone.

A view of Braodmoor Farm showing two horses pulling the hay cart on South Meadow in the 1920s, with Jack Eustice on the cart. South Meadow is now part of a large housing development.

Broadmoor School, 1915. Back row, left to right: Harold Woodley, Lilly Donnelly, Nancy Donnelly, Gertie Stokes, Sid Cotterel, Joe Cotterel, Margaret Sale, Mabel Woodley, Jack Edwards, Ivy Sale. Middle row: Alice Spicer, Florence Stokes, Eve Jeans, Florie Greenough, Reg Goodwin, Edie Spicer, Olive Barnett, Mabel Jeans. Front row: Alan Edwards, Tommy Lee, George Donnelly, Mara Cotterel, Bertha Stokes, Charlie Greenough, Phyllis Jeans, Mary Barnet, Doris Sale, Teddy Coombs.

Broadmoor Avenue, Crowthorne which led out into the High Street. The Iron Duke is on the opposite side of the road

Lower Broadmoor Road, Crowthorne, showing staff houses used as accommodation for families whose members worked at Broadmoor.

The railings on the left continue from Broadmoor Avenue and show the road leading to Sandhurst in 1885 with Wellington Villas on the right.

View of the road from Sandhurst to Crowthorne near the Mordaunt Gate, looking towards Crowthorne, 1885.

View from the bend on the hill approaching Crowthorne, 1921. The footpath on the right led through the woods to Little Sandhurst.

Site of the sawmills, showing equipment, the horse that was used for hauling logs and the men who worked in Cox's Wood. Cox's Wood, now known as Edgbarrow Wood, was on the left on the road to Sandhurst.

Cox's Wood, showing two men with pole wagons collecting wood in 1887.

Edgbarrow Cottage, with the horse and cart outside, surrounded by Cox's Wood. The house is still there today, deep in the woods.

Acknowledgements

We would like to thank all those people who have helped us to compile this selection of photographs; also Mrs Sylvia Trevis for doing all the typing, Mr Wells of M.J.W. Photographic, for copying the pictures, and Mr Sopwith from Wellington College for his special help with pictures and information.

Mrs Adkins • Mrs Ambrose • Mr Barson • Mr Bell • Mr Bennett
Berkshire County Council • Mr Brooker • Mr Bryant • Mr Burnham
Camberley News • Catholic Chapel RMA • Catholic church, Crowthorne
Catholic church, Sandhurst • Mr Clark • Mr G. Clarke • Mrs Cornish
Mrs Cox • Mr Cumnor • Mr and Mrs Curtis • Mrs Dancy • Mrs Dean
Miss Edgington • Miss Eyres • Mrs Goswell • Mrs Greenfield • Mr Greenfield
Mr Holmes • Mr Hayward • Mrs Hatfield • Mrs Hampton • Mrs Hill
Mr Ironside • Miss Johnson • Edward Jones • Mr Kane • Mr Keep
Kempthorne album • Mr Kibbey • Mrs Liddiard • Mr and Mrs Loader
Miss Lumber • Mr and Miss Lyford • Misses Mason • Mrs McCandles
Mr Moth • Miss Newman • Mrs Newman • Mrs Pace • Mrs Patterson
Mr Pearmain • Mrs Piper • Mr Purvey • Mr Rance • Reading University
Mr Rogers • Mrs Rudkin • Sandhurst Museum • Sandhurst Women's Institute
Mrs Sargeant • Mrs Score • Mrs Searle • Miss Seeby • Dr D. Shepherd
Mr Sinnot • Miss G. Stokes • Mr and Mrs Stubley • Mrs Vaughan
Misses Watkins • Wellington College Archives • Mrs Willis • Mr Young